MY LIFE

Dilip Kumar

GP Editors

GENERAL PRESS

Published by
GENERAL PRESS
4805/24, Fourth Floor, Krishna House
Ansari Road, Daryaganj, New Delhi - 110002
Ph : 011-23282971, 45795759
E-mail : generalpressindia@gmail.com

www.generalpress.in

© General Press

All rights reserved. No part of this publication may be reproduced, stored in a retrieval system, or transmitted, in any form or by any means—electronic, mechanical, photocopying, recording or otherwise—without the prior written permission of the publishers.

First Edition : 2018

ISBN : 9789388118934

Purchase our Books and eBooks online from:
Amazon.in | Flipkart.com | Play Store

Published by Azeem Ahmad Khan for General Press

Contents

Introduction 5

1. Childhood 11
2. Bombay 23
3. Poona 31
4. Bombay Talkies 39
5. Personal Life 53
6. Lesser Known Facts about Dilip Kumar 67
7. Filmography 75

Introduction

I don't believe you have to be better than everybody else. I believe you have to be better than you ever thought you could be.

—Dilip Kumar

Dev Anand, Raj Kapoor and Dilip Kumar were contemporaries of each other, during the time India was at its peak with its struggle for Independence. Dilip Kumar was born Mohammad Yusuf Khan—to Ayesha Begum and Lala Ghulam Sarwar Ali Khan in a Muslim Hindko-speaking Awan family. For most of his childhood, he lived in Peshawar, North West Frontier Province. His father was a landlord and a fruit merchant, and he owned orchards in Peshawar and Deolali. Young Yusuf grew up in a joint family, where his *Dadi* had a tyrannical rule over the whole household.

He moved to Bombay when his father came back after a brief stint in the upcoming city and realizing it offered a lot of opportunities. While his *Dadi* wasn't too keen on the idea, for once his Dada stood firm in his decision to let the wife and children live with their husband and father! After finishing his college education, Yusuf left his home in a huff after a disagreement with his father. He arrived at Poona (now Pune) and that was his first tryst with earning his own keep. He recalls having left his house with just forty rupees in his pocket!

His coming into what we now know as Bollywood was quite accidental. He just happened to be at the right place at the right time and Devika Rani saw what Yusuf had never seen in himself—untapped potential. Since the pay was quite good, he decided to go ahead and give this profession a shot.

It was his movie *Jugnu* with its huge hoardings that gave him the first taste of stardom. The movie posters were hung all around the town, and clued his father in about what he had been secretly indulging in.

Dilip Kumar was not always spared of controversy. Despite television not being a medium during his initial Bollywood days, there were snoopy journalists all around. He and his co-actors conducted themselves in public. His affair with Madhubala was widely publicized and there have been many accounts of their breakup—with each party holding onto their side of the story. The fact remains Dilip Kumar

married Saira Banu and they have been an indomitable team for years to come.

Dilip Kumar had ruled Bollywood during his days by adopting a screen name because he didn't want to associate his family name in this business as his father wasn't too happy about his decision to join the *nautanki* business.

Chapter 1

Childhood

Yusuf Khan was born on 11th December 1922 to his parents, Ayesha Begum and Lala Ghulam Sarwar Ali Khan, in Peshawar, North West Frontier Province, British India. In today's world it is known as Khyber Pakhtunkhwa, Pakistan. That day went down in history not because India's future superstar had been born but because there had been a fire outbreak in the Goldsmith's Lane. His father was amongst the many people who went out to help. While his *Chacha Umeer* fetched the midwife, and waited in agony for the arrival of the bundle who would become Dilip Kumar later on in his life! He was one of the twelve children of his parents, and spent his childhood days in Peshawar under the rule of his tyrannical *Dadi*.

While he used to be a happy young boy, things changed when a fakir visited their house when he was five years old and declared that he was made for the stuff of the legends! His *Dadi* took the fakir's words seriously and shaved off poor little Yusuf's lovely hair. She also took too making his face ashen so as to keep him away from the evil eye.

His appearance made him the center of ridicule for all of his schoolmates and he did not make any friends in school. It was his older brother who was senior to him by just a year, Ayub Saab, who served as his friend and confidant throughout his life.

While his parents understood that his *Dadi* had the best interest for him at heart, they failed to understand that the constant bullying and constant shying away from attention made Yusuf into an introvert. He receded into his own shell, and followed his mother, his beloved *Ammi* around like a shadow.

He recounts his growing up days in Peshawar as constantly looking for adventure while the whole house would nap during the afternoon. Often these were misadventures and he found himself in the wrong place at the wrong time. This led to him once witnessing a dead boy as it lay there eerily still and being almost caught by their household help, Ghani. In his own autobiography, Dilip Kumar muses about how full moon nights used to be exceptionally hard for Ghani. Nevertheless, he was an indispensable asset for the family because he could keep the thieves away from their precious supplies. Especially during the times of war when the NWFP got cut off and Yusuf's father suffered losses.

Despite being annoyed with his *Dadi* because of the horrible appearance she forced him to keep, Yusuf knew that she was one of his favourites. She would always wear a shawl, and during the times he needed a place to hide from his parents she would open up her arms and let him seek refuge under the folds of her shawl. It always astounded him to think that she could fit so many things under the giant folds of her shawl! Nevertheless, he could go undiscovered for quite some time—thanks to his *Dadi's* generosity.

Although quite young, Yusuf noticed there was a difference in the way the daughters and the daughter-in-laws of the house were treated. It was a matriarchy but his *Ammi* was the one who was given the sole responsibility of the kitchen. He would watch her toil away all day long in the kitchen. Even when Yusuf's father, *Aghaji*, would point out the unfairness to his mother, *Ammi* would hush him. She would claim it was because no one could match her skills in making the savories that go along with the endless pots of tea she would keep making. His mother would be so exhausted by her chores, that by night time she would sleep like a log.

Yusuf noticed that none of his *buas* would help her out in the kitchen, except *Phoopi Babjani,* who was extremely fond of his mother and would sometimes help her out. She would even yell at her mother for making Ayesha work so hard. But *Dadi* remained firm in her stance that she was doing nothing wrong!

Things were not great for Yusuf in school. But he was fluent in Urdu, Pushtu and also English. This was a source of pride for his father, and often times he would find himself being forced to perform poems he'd learned in school in front of audiences paying rapt attention to him. He was a huge hit with all his family members due to his willingness to pass from one aunt to another, while his mother completed all the menial household work.

Winters in Peshawar were especially bitter. Every family therefore kept Persian cats that were made to sleep on the beds to keep them warm for the human occupants later on in the day. In the terrace of the Khan's household, they would often hold entertainment such as playing *antakshari* and reciting *shaayeri*. They would often have to follow the themes that were decided upon during the beginning of the night. Young Yusuf would be passed on from relative to relative, and often he would wonder in the morning how he had ended up in the place he did! His *Dadi* was adamant about the quality of stories that would be shared in these sessions. All the stories shared would have to have a moral. Sometimes she would cut someone's performance off if she felt that the quality wasn't what she wanted the children of the family to hear.

During his childhood, Yusuf remembers his mother's mother and sister visiting their house in their horse drawn carriages. It was obvious that his mother hailed from a very well to do family, and her family would always come bearing gifts for everyone in the family. It broke Yusuf's heart to watch his frail mother toil day in and day out. The only time he truly saw his mother relax and have fun was when she went back home for her sister's wedding. He noted how everyone fussed over her. It was during that brief stay at his *Ammi's maiyka* that he was spared having to ashen his face. He was relieved and enjoyed himself during the festivities. He was always trying to find ways to make his *Ammi's* life better.

Young Yusuf also noted that his parents never shouted at one another. Whatever their differences might have been, they were always sorted out quietly and calmly. It was not in either of his parents' natures to create a ruckus, as had been his *Dadi*, and his eldest sister, Sakina's nature. He never saw Sakina lend a hand to her mother in the kitchen. But she would never let go off an opportunity to get into a fight with her. His mother for the most part avoided getting into any kind of quarrels with her.

He also noticed that his father never failed to bring back something special for his wife from his many trips. She would take it quietly from him in the privacy of their room, and lock it away in her almirah, never making a big deal of the fact she was given a gift by her husband.

Yusuf wasn't the most studious child but he did passably well in his studies. His English education was further fuelled by attending Barnes School, Deolali, Nashik. As mentioned before, his father was mighty proud of his son and it was his dream to see him in a profession which would allow him to prefix OBE (Order of the British Empire) to his name.

Neither father nor son knew what was going to happen in a few years when the son decided to follow in Raj Kapoor's footsteps and enter the entertainment business!

Chapter 2

Bombay

Bombay, present day Mumbai, was known even back then as the land of opportunities. *Aghaji* came to explore the opportunities that this new city would provide as his fruit business started suffering due to the war raging on, and the North West Frontier Province getting cut off because of the supplies.

He decided to come back and move his entire family into this new city. While *Dadi* opposed this idea, believing the family should stay on with them in Peshawar, *Dada* did not agree with the view. He wanted the family to stay together especially since he knew how much *Aghaji* was missing his wife and children. They went off to the new land, and this was where Yusuf spent most of his adolescence.

In Bombay, young Yusuf also witnessed a love story brewing between his eldest brother, Noor Saab, and the neighbour's daughter. Being the younger sibling, he was forced to obey the orders dished out by his brother. Sometimes he was asked to bring little notes to the girl. She would accept them and give him a sweet or a toffee as a reward, ruffling his hair. For young Yusuf, it was fun to make his brother jump out of his skin by doubling back as soon as he could after running his errand in record time! The girl would find this hilarious and they would see her laughing. However, Noor Saab's love story got nipped in the bud when *Ammi* caught Yusuf eating sweets and asked him where those came from! Not being one to lie to his mother, Yusuf ended up spilling the beans about the secret love affair and Noor Saab was taken to task. The girl next door got married to someone else in another city. The families still greeted each other cordially, as though nothing had ever happened between them.

It was in Khalsa College that he got reacquainted with Raj Kapoor. They had always been friends, even as little kids they grew up in the same neighbourhood initially. People often think they were only friends because they ended up in the same profession, but the truth is Yusuf and Raj had been friends for a lifetime, even before bumping into each other at the same studios!

People commuted by trams in those olden days before it got replaced by the Mumbai local trains. His family lived near Churchgate, and Yusuf found it fairly easy to travel. His school had been a walking distance for him. In college he was reunited with Raj Kapoor, and he had on several occasion tried to break Yusuf out of his shy and reserved behaviour with women.

Bombay was indeed a city which offered a lot of opportunities. *Aghaji's* business flourished, and he did not have to go to the market often because he had employed people who would take care of the daily chores for him. Instead, he spent a lot of time at home, in the company of his family and friends. Since everyone loved this family, it was never devoid of visitors. However endless visitors meant that *Ammi* kept toiling away at the kitchen. Yusuf was also in awe of the way in which they settled down in their new abode and she had become quite popular with her neighbours. It remained a mystery to everyone as to how she communicated with her new friends for they did not speak a word of Pushtu and she did not speak a word of Hindi! Yet they could get their thoughts communicated to each other without missing a beat!

During his college days, Yusuf enjoyed playing football and it was his dream to make it one of the big leagues, and play the sport professionally. However, it was cricket that dominated the country. While he dreamed of playing the sport professionally, Yusuf's father still dreamed of seeing his son going places in his life. But to him that meant getting employed in a government job and have the OBE to his name. Yusuf was going to inherit the family business was a given, since Noor did not show any interest in it, and Ayub was always too ill to do anything. In fact, Noor was pretty backwards in his outlooks. He did not support his father's decision to give access to education to the daughters of the house. He did not see the need to let the womenfolk go to college to study the subjects that they were interested in. He did not believe that women needed to be educated! Yusuf and Noor never did see eye to eye about anything.

Ayub's ill health had kept him away from school. He was homeschooled however, and was proficient in both Urdu and English. In fact, Ayub would dabble in Urdu poetry that they discussed at length at times. Ayub was hardly a year older to Yusuf, and they got along like a house on fire. He was also the only person who Yusuf confided in when he needed someone to talk to. In many ways, they were each other's friends. One of their childhood memories was hiding coins under a loose tile in their home in Peshawar, which their *Dada* had claimed would double over time for there was magic. Of course nothing of that sort ever happened, and when they went back to their ancestral home they figured out that their *Dada* had pulled a trick on them! It broke their hearts to think he was not amongst them laughing at how innocently these two fell for his tricks.

Ayub's condition worsened when he fell from his horse during a business trip with his father in Kashmir, where they had gone to further their fruit business. This fall left him paralyzed and bed ridden for a year! During this time Yusuf would read Urdu poetry to him, and be his constant companion. *Ammi* and Ayub were moved to Deolali for fresh air and hopes of a quick recovery for him. While he did recover over time, he never did gain back the strength that he once had. Being sickly from the beginning made the odds against him higher. Yusuf was constantly under the threat of losing his brother. It is obvious from his memoir, that Ayub Saab reserved a very special place in Yusuf's heart.

Chapter 3

Poona

Incidentally, when Yusuf left his home for the first time as a teenager, after a fight with his father, he did not contact anyone except his dear brother Ayub. Of course he did not contact Ayub first off. He took a third class ticket because he needed to spare out the forty odd rupees that was in his pocket when he left his home.

His father had always provided him and his siblings with the best of everything. During the time Yusuf was trying to fend for himself, he realized how much his father worked to make sure his children received the best of everything. For starters, they all had first class season tickets for their tram and later train rides. His father wanted nothing but the best for his sons and daughters. Yusuf chose to go to Poona to try his luck because he knew he wouldn't be able to pull off that stunt in Mumbai. Too many people knew his father, and the news he was trying to look for a job would no doubt reach back to him. It would have broken his father's heart to learn that his son was trying to look for a job that he considered beyond his dignity!

Poona offered anonymity that Mumbai did not to Yusuf, who still did not know that much greater things waited for him in the horizon. Little did he know that he was going to be known as the Tragedy King in the years to come! For now, a boy on the threshold of manhood, Yusuf was struggling to make ends meet. He met a nice Parsi-couple who owned a café and wanted to know where he might find some work. Because he could speak well and was quiet conversant in English, he was hired by the manager of the Army Canteen. He knew about the various shady dealings that was going on between the manager and the vendors, but feigned ignorance about the same. In return, the manager allowed him to set up his own sandwich stall. The regulars at the Army Canteen were delighted with the delicacies he had to offer, and he sold out everything he had brought. Others who came in later were disappointed to learn that they had missed quite the treat. This continued for a few years. Once he had enough money, he sent a money order back home to Ayub Saab, informing him that he was fine and of his whereabouts. The very next day, Ayub arrived to meet his brother. Yusuf did not go back with him, but they were both pleased with their reunion.

While Yusuf's father wanted him to take over the family business, Yusuf couldn't help but feel that he was meant for bigger things. Maybe the words of fakir had lingered in his mind longer and impacted him deeper than he had believed. He always felt something was missing and he was meant for bigger things than following in his father's profession.

He had quite the colourful experience in Poona. He even spent a night in jail with Gandhi ji's supporters after he was arrested for airing anti-British views. In truth, he had just been asked to speak his mind about the current state of affairs in the country. It was during the time when India was fight for her Independence the most, the non-violence and civil disobedience movements were at their peak. Of course he was bailed out of jail but he felt proud about sharing the same space as Gandhi ji's followers. It was also enough for him to retire his solo life and go home to his family.

Only Ayub Saab knew the exact date on which his brother was coming home. He kept that a secret to surprise their *Ammi*. During his stint at Poona, Yusuf had managed to save Rs. 5,000. He was mighty proud of himself and he planned to surprise his mother with the money. Things did not go according to his plan however. His mother was overjoyed to be reunited with her son, but when he gave her the money, she was extremely concerned about its origins. She got out the *Quraan* and made him swear on the Holy Book that he had not acquired this money by any dishonest means. While his mother questioning, his honesty stung him, Yusuf obliged and that satisfied his mother. His father, on the other hand, welcome in back as though nothing had changed between them. Yusuf was aware that if had given it sometime, his mother would have fixed things between them. But he was hot-headed and he wanted to make his own way in the world. He tried, and he was a success at it. But since he always longed to do bigger and better things, he came back. After all, he was the prodigal son of the household. And amazing things were expected of him in any case.

Chapter 4

Bombay Talkies

Even though Raj Kapoor, his friend for many years, was in the entertainment industry, Yusuf never really thought about going into the business himself. His launch into the industry was quiet by accident. He bumped into Dr. Masani at the Churchgate station. Yusuf had been on his way to Dadar in order to meet someone for business. Upon learning that Yusuf was looking for a job, he offered to let Yusuf accompany him to Bombay Talkies, a film studio in Malad,

where he was headed. He was of the opinion that there might be something or the other that would suit Yusuf's criteria quite nicely.

Knowing that he had nothing to lose and there was no harm in trying, Yusuf joined Dr. Masani on his trip to Bombay Talkies. This would become the day when everything changed in his life. The owner of the studio, Devika Rani, was so taken by Yusuf's good looks that when asked if there was a job available for him she asked him if he would like to become an actor. She offered him a monthly salary of Rs. 1250

which was more than generous in those days. She later admitted that she offered that amount so that he could readily get onboard. Yusuf was convinced he had misheard her since he was certain that Raj Kapoor was employed with a monthly salary of Rs. 170. He did tell her that he knew nothing about acting but that did not deter her, since she was of the opinion that anyone willing to learn and put in the hard work could become an actor.

He readily accepted the offer, and informed his family that he was gainfully employed. He avoided telling anyone except Ayub about the true nature of his employment. He knew his family needed all the extra money since two of his aunts had taken up permanent residence with them, and it wasn't easy taking care of so many people. He often wondered why his other brothers never stepped up to take more responsibility for the family, to ease their father from his role of being the breadwinner of the family. Even when his success went through the roof, and his father could happily retire, he did not.

Because he did not want Yusuf be the only earning member of the family. He wanted to contribute whatever little he could to the family.

Raj Kapoor was surprised to find his friend from college in the Bombay Talkies Studio. He welcomed his friend and showed him the ropes around the place. Soon young Yusuf was amongst the company of eminent film personalities such as Ashok Kumar, S. Mukherjiet al. In fact, his knowledge of the Urdu language made them ask him to help with the dialogues since most of the writers of the studio were Bengali and struggled with the language. Yusuf's inputs were most welcomed by them. Soon, he was brainstorming with the writers and bettering their dialogues. They gladly welcomed his suggestions and he started feeling right at home with his colleagues at Bombay Talkies.

Devika Rani summoned Yusuf not long before he started shooting for his first movie. She said thoughtfully that he might want to think about adopting a screen name that his viewers would be comfortable with. She was the one who suggested Dilip Kumar, since that name had popped up in her head and she believed it had a nice ring to it. He was quite speechless about adopting a whole new persona, but he knew he would have to do that in order to keep his family name intact. Ashok Kumar put his mind at ease saying even he had to adopt a screen name, but to everyone in Bombay Talkies he would always be Yusuf. That helped him come to his decision quicker. Ashok Kumar was also the one who taught him the trick of not acting, but actually being in the moment and imitating real life. He watched Ashok Kumar's shooting and learned whatever he could about the craft.

His first shot where he had to run proved to be a disaster since he ran too fast and all the camera caught was a blur. As was the culture with Bombay Talkies, they did countless rehearsals until they were absolutely certain that everything would be exactly as they imagined in the final cut. Both Devika Rani and Ashok Kumar made Yusuf understand that he could ask for a retake if he wasn't satisfied with the shot. It was an actor's job to deliver his best possible performance. Sometimes the scripts, no matter how detailed, did not tell you what the character might be feeling in the moment. So the actor had to really step up his game to make a strong impact.

Jwar Bhata was Dilip Kumar's debut movie. It did not do as well as had been predicted. In fact, it was until *Jugnu* that anyone sat up to take any notice of this newcomer. Dilip Kumar had already witnessed stardom closely when he travelled with Ashok Kumar. But he noticed how casually and normally he spoke with his fans. And despite the success of *Kismet*, and with everything else going on, the man remained grounded firmly to his reality. This made Dilip Kumar focus and never lose sight of his own personal goals.

His father eventually found out about his profession, when Raj Kapoor's grandfather paid him a visit and dragged him out to see a huge poster for *Jugnu* hanging over Crawford Market. Although disappointed in his son's choice of career, he didn't say anything to him. Finally, it was a visit from Prithviraj Kapoor to the house, that helped smooth things over between father-son. Dilip Kumar had turned to his friend, Raj Kapoor, during his hours of need. Raj had always known that things would go south when *Aghaji* eventually found out about the reality of what Yusuf had been up to all those days.

He finally came to terms with Dilip's choice of profession when he visited a relative's house and they were singing praises about his son. While he didn't necessarily like his son's choice, he respected it and finally went to the theatre to watch his son on the giant screen with *Umeer Chacha*. It was the movie *Mela* that they went to see, and while his *Chacha Umeer* praised his performance, his father said if he really wanted to marry that girl he would go in person and speak to her family. Dilip was naturally confused at first and then he realized that his father to had confused the reel with the real! He explained to his father that they were all playing different characters on screen and in real life there was nothing more than friendship between him and the leading lady, Nargis. He feared that if didn't explain this to his *Aghaji* at once, he would honestly hunt down Nargis and send a marriage proposal on his son's behalf.

The happiness that Dilip Kumar's success must have brought was marred by him losing his beloved brother to ill health. During his last days, Ayub requested to be taken to Marine Drive, and they sat, talking and discussing Urdu poetry or in silence. Yusuf's mother passed away soon after Independence, and that was a blow that Yusuf never could get over. She could not deal with losing Ayub and though she never cried in front of the family, her pillow would be wet with her tears at night, crying softly over the loss of her beloved son.

Independence also meant that there was no longer a ban on the kind of movies the studios could make. Slowly the monthly employment scheme of studios were going to get replaced. Devika Rani was moving away from Mumbai, and Dilip Kumar's contract with Bombay Talkies was coming to an end. Now, a new system was developed wherein an agency would mediate between an actor, director and studio, and each would be hired on a freelance basis.

This setup was a welcome change because it meant that actors could now work with other directors as well, and were not restricted to the same studios. They were able to explore more avenues. For Dilip Kumar, it was a welcome change. As it was for Indian cinema.

Chapter 5

Personal Life

It took longer for Dilip Kumar to gain success as an actor. He had his own shares of ups and downs. But nevertheless, his perseverance got him there. He started getting the recognition and adulation that had been due to him for a long time. He was mighty young when he took up the job of acting.

He was beginning to blur the lines between the real and reel, since he kept playing tragic character roles despite barely being in his twenties. He even consulted a psychiatrist, namely Dr. Nichols, who told him that his problem wasn't an uncommon one. A lot of actors faced the same issues he did, playing the same kind of roles and obsessing over the characters, long after his job was done at the studios. He was even suggested that he should take a break from his serious roles and try his hand at some other genre—something completely different from what he dabbled in—like perhaps comedy.

While most of the people in industry advised him against it, Mukherji Saab encouraged him and he was asked to try his hand at comedy by K. Asif. During that time, Sriramulu Naidu had approached him to remake the Tamil movie, *Malaikallan,* and Dilip Kumar had taken up the project. It was going to be his first role in comedy, and *Azaad* proved to be a huge success. Even though Dilip Kumar had gone off to a hill station, Mahabaleshwar, to escape the initial thoughts and reactions of his family and friends. He need not have worried because the movie

was a huge success, and managed to put the minds of everyone involved at peace. This included Meena Kumari, who too got a welcome break from becoming a stereotype.

Often in his autobiography Dilip Kumar mentions that sometimes he could not get the temperature right with his leading lady. It had happened for him in *Tarana* with Madhubala. But he could never achieve that with Nargis. Raj Kapoor, on the other hand, could get that temperature right with Nargis. He had seen the same happen with Ashok Kumar and Kamini Kaushal. Needless to say, these temperatures could be achieved if the actors felt something towards each other even after the cameras had stopped rolling. Dilip Kumar had been asked, as had almost everyone in Bollywood, if there really was something going on between him and his co-stars. A movie always does well especially if the viewers' think that there is something brewing between their beloved actors. People tend to blur the reel with the real, as do actors when they stay in their characters skins for too long.

It is not a secret that Madhubala was in love with Dilip Kumar. He returned these feelings. He was amused when she sent him a rose with a note, and asked him to accept it if he felt the same way about her. She was young and vivacious when she entered the film industry. However, their marriage never took place because the marriage proposal sent forth by her father to Dilip felt more like a business deal than anything else. Dilip felt accepting that would stunt his growth in the film industry. Madhubala claimed that this was not true and all her father ever wanted was for him to apologize. This was for the court case against Madhubala and her father, against the Chopras. Dilip Kumar had chosen the Chopra's side. Madhubala remained in love with him for many years despite their breakup. She ended up marrying Kishore Kumar, which stunned everyone who knew her. Even after her death, there were rumours of spotting Dilip Kumar at her grave.

It was actress Saira Banu who Dilip Kumar married on 11th October 1966. She was 22 years his junior, but she was the kind of person that Dilip wanted to spend the rest of his life with. He was loved by her family, and it was of no surprise that the marriage had been readily agreed upon. While his eldest sister disapproved of this match because she was an actress, Dilip stood firm in his decision. His youngest brother, Naseer, was also extremely pleased with this match.

Both Saira and Dilip were happy to be married. Saira insisted on staying together with the family, because she did not want to separate them. Dilip's successful film allowed him to buy a bungalow in Pali Hill, Bandra. It had been his dream to buy a house for his beloved *Ammi*, so that she could have a place that she would call her home. She passed away before he could achieve this feat.

Luckily, he found a loving and understanding partner in Saira. She was the one who encouraged him years later to write his autobiography, especially after he came across a book that go the details about his life wrong.

His marriage to Saira was a happy one. They continued working together even after marriage in films, and he recalls how he tried to help his wife deliver the best performances. They were expecting a baby in 1972, but they lost the baby. Thinking it was the Divine's Will, they abandoned trying to have kids. It was an information that Dilip Kumar chose to reveal in his autobiography.

During the brief time from 1981-1983 he was married to the socialite, Asma Sahiba. That news shocked the entire world since no one expected Dilip Kumar to do something this scandalous! That marriage ended, however, even though it was quite difficult to dissolve. Saira's faith in her husband was gone and she later gave an interview in which she said she didn't see dreams in broad daylight anymore. Once upon a time her dream was to be Mrs. Dilip Kumar, but it had turned into a nightmare during the month of October 1982! Dilip's family did not mind his second wife, and she was installed at his Pali Hill residence. However, Saira forced him to choose between her and the new wife. Dilip chose his wife of sixteen years—but he lost her confidence in him forever. He also chooses not to talk about this episode, claiming he tried to do the honorable thing by marrying Asma.

Dilip Kumar does not have any heirs. His nephew, Ayub, has two children—who are the heirs to the Khan-Kumar family. He is fluent in Urdu, Hindi,

Hindko, Bhojpuri, English, Bengali, Pashto and Farsi. Having a flair for language, he used to pick them up whenever he interacted with people who predominantly spoke those languages!

Dilip Kumar was also involved in a number of humanitarian work. He had planned and conceptualized the famous Jogger's Park in Bandra, along with Sunil Dutt and Oliver Andrade.

Despite of his successful film career, Dilip Kumar, suffered many losses over the course of his life. Losing his brothers, Ayub and Naseer had not been easy for him. He still recalls keeping the news of Naseer's death away from Saira, lest he make her ill once again. She was in recovery during the time of his accident. Losing his *Ammi* was particularly heartbreaking for him as well. He says that every death was equally damming for him, and he takes time to come to terms with the fact that the people he spent all his life with, even the people who he worked with are no more! This list includes Mehboob Saab, Ashok Kumar, and Raj Kapoor among others.

Today at ninety-five, he continues living in his Pali Hill bungalow in Bandra with his wife. He has lived his full life and watched Bollywood grow into a place that was more accepting of other people.

It certainly is a place where people can now enter without changing their names, to match their audiences' sentiments. In fact, in today's world, Bollywood is being dominated by the Khans. In fact, if young Yusuf Khan were to be launched today—he wouldn't need to change his name at all.

Chapter 6

Lesser Known Facts about Dilip Kumar

- Dilip Kumar acted in a total of 60 films plus 3 guest appearances and four uncredited appearances in 54 years. (1944-1998).

- He has never acted in more than 2-3 films in a year—hitting the peak at the very beginning with 5 films in 1948!

- Dilip Kumar's most productive years were between 1948-1961 when he acted in 31 different films!

- Between 1964 and 1976, he worked in only 14 films.

- As a character actor, between 1981 and 1998 he has just 14 releases.

- He was awarded the 'Dadasaheb Phalke Lifetime Achievement Award' in 1995.

- He has never won the National Award for Best Actor.

- He was paired opposite to Nargis and Vyjayanthimala (6 times each). The others: Nimmi (5 times), Kamini Kaushal, Madhubala, Meena Kumari, Waheeda Rehman and Saira Banu (4 times each). He was paired only twice with the actress he admired the most: Nalini Jaywant.

- He was never paired opposite Suraiya though they were set to work together in a film named

Janwar, which was to have been directed by K. Asif.

- He acted opposite Nutan in his later films, *Karma* and *Kanoon Apna Apna*. He also starred opposite Rekha in his last two films, *Qila* and *Aag Ka Dariya*.

- Dilip Kumar has acted opposite both his contemporaries as least once: Raj Kapoor in *Andaaz* and Dev Anand in *Insaniyat*. He acted twice with Raaj Kumar—in *Paigham* and *Saudagar*, as with Sanjeev Kumar—in *Sunghursh* and later *Vidhaata*.

- Dilip Kumar was very choosy about his onscreen appearances. Once, Dilip Kumar had refused to work with Nargis in *Mother India*. While the film became one of the most memorable ones in the history of Indian cinema, the actor had his own reasons to not be a part of the film.

- He acted in nine films with Pran, known for playing the villain.

- He was offered the nine roles of *Naya Din Nayi Raat* which was later played by Sanjeev Kumar, as he refused and settled to speak the commentary.

- In 2004, a digitally restored and colourised version of *Mughal-E-Azam* with Dolby sound was released.

- *Bairaag* was Dilip Kumar's last film as the conventional leading man. This was his brother, Naseer Khan's last film as well. It was, however, stage performer, Kader Khan's first film.

Chapter 7

Filmography

Year	Film	Role	Awards
1944	Jwar Bhata	Jagdish	
1945	Pratima		
1946	Milan	Ramesh	
1947	Jugnu	Sooraj	
1948	Shaheed	Ram	
1948	Nadiya Ke Paar		
1948	Mela	Mohan	
1948	Ghar Ki Izzat	Chanda	
1948	Anokha Pyar	Ashok	
1949	Shabnam	Manoj	
1949	Andaz	Dilip	
1950	Jogan	Vijay	

1950	*Babul*	Ashok	
1950	*Arzoo*	Badal	
1951	*Tarana*	Motilal	
1951	*Hulchul*	Kishore	
1951	*Deedaar*	Shamu	
1952	*Sangdil*	Shankar	
1952	*Daag*	Shankar	Filmfare Award for Best Actor
1952	*Aan*	Jai Tilak	
1953	*Chandirani*	Kishore	
1953	*Shikast*	Dr. Ram Singh	
1953	*Footpath*	Noshu	
1954	*Amar*	Amarnath	
1955	*Azaad*		Filmfare Award for Best Actor
1955	*Uran Khatola*		
1955	*Insaniyat*	Mangal	

Year	Film	Role	Award
1955	*Devdas*	Devdas	Filmfare Award for Best Actor
1957	*Naya Daur*	Shankar	Filmfare Award for Best Actor
1957	*Musafir*		
1958	*Yahudi*	Prince Marcus	
1958	*Madhumati*	Anand/Deven	Nominated - Filmfare Award for Best Actor
1959	*Paighaam*	Ratan Lal	Nominated - Filmfare Award for Best Actor
1960	*Kohinoor*	Yuvraj Rana Devendra Bahadur	Filmfare Award for Best Actor
1960	*Mughal-E-Azam*	Prince Saleem	
1961	*Gunga Jumna*	Gunga	Nominated - Filmfare Award for Best Actor
1964	*Leader*	Vijay Khanna	Filmfare Award for Best Actor

1966	*Dil Diya Dard Liya*	Shankar/ Rajasaheb	Nominated - Filmfare Award for Best Actor
1967	*Ram Aur Shyam*	Ram/Shyam (Dual Role)	Filmfare Award for Best Actor
1968	*Sunghursh*		Nominated - Filmfare Award for Best Actor
1968	*Aadmi*	Rajesh/ Raja Saheb	Nominated - Filmfare Award for Best Actor
1970	*Sagina Mahato*	Sagina	
1970	*Gopi*	Gopi	Nominated - Filmfare Award for Best Actor
1972	*Dastaan*	Anil/Sunil (Dual Role)	
1972	*Anokha Milan*		
1974	*Sagina*		Nominated - Filmfare Award for Best Actor
1974	*Phir Kab Milogi*		

Year	Film	Role	Award
1976	Bairaag	Kailash/ Bholenath/ Sanjay (Triple Role)	Nominated - Filmfare Award for Best Actor
1981	Kranti	Sanga/Kranti	
1982	Vidhaata	Shamsher Singh	
1982	Shakti	Ashvini Kumar	Filmfare Award for Best Actor
1983	Mazdoor	Dinanath Saxena	
1984	Duniya	Mohan Kumar	
1984	Mashaal	Vinod Kumar	Nominated - Filmfare Award for Best Actor
1986	Dharm Adhikari	Dharam Raj	
1986	Karma	Vishwanath Pratap Singh, alias Rana	
1989	Kanoon Apna Apna	Collector Jagat Pratap Singh	
1990	Izzatdaar	Brahma Dutt	

1990	*Aag Ka Dariya*		
1991	*Saudagar*	Thakur Veer Singh	Nominated - Filmfare Award for Best Actor
1998	*Qila*	Jaganath/ Amarnath Singh (Dual Role)	

www.ingramcontent.com/pod-product-compliance
Lightning Source LLC
Chambersburg PA
CBHW051349040426
42453CB00007B/483